Accept the Cards

Sometimes,
The best thing you can do is not to think about what could have been.
Just accept the cards that have been dealt.
What's meant to be,
will be.

Fragments of Us

Brittany Benko

Published by Brittany Benko, 2024.

While every precaution has been taken in the preparation of this book, the publisher assumes no responsibility for errors or omissions, or for damages resulting from the use of the information contained herein.

FRAGMENTS OF US

First edition. November 1, 2024.

Copyright © 2024 Brittany Benko.

ISBN: 979-8227654731

Written by Brittany Benko.

Also by Brittany Benko

Poetic Poetry: A Short Collection of Poems
Poetic Poems and Prose
The Guiding Pen
Fragments of Us

Watch for more at https://brittanybenko.wixsite.com/booksbybrittany.

Table of Contents

Actions 1

Afraid 2

Back Together 3

Beating Heart 4

Biggest Burden 5

Bloomed Anew 6

Daily Tears 7

Deserving Love 8

Distant Hum 9

Farewell 10

Favorite Regret 11

Field of Thorns 12

Fight 13

Finding Myself 14

Foolish Love 15

Fragments of Light 16

Garden of my Heart 17

Hardest Lesson 18

Hating Myself 19

Heartbroken 20

Home of Silence 21

Hope 22

Hopeful Pain 23

I Rise 24

I Will Miss You 25

I'm Healing 26

Intense Pain 27

Lessons 28

Letting Go 29

Life 30

Loneliness 31

Lost Relationship 32
Lost Star 33
Love 34
Love Lesson 35
Loving You 36
Memory 37
Mosaic of Strength 38
Navigating Sorrow 39
New Beginnings 40
Nightmare of Reality 41
Not at Fault 42
Old Love Letter 43
Plastered Smile 44
Reliving Pain 45
Resilience 46
Rough Waters 47
Saying Goodbye 48
Shattered Love 49
Shipwreck 50
Slipping Away 51
Stark Reality 52
Storm of Chaos 53
Strangers 54
Struggling 55
Struggling Heart 56
Stuck 57
Tempest of Tears 58
Thank You 59
The Wrong Person 60
There for You 61
Tragedy 62
Two Souls 63
Unwavering Beauty 64

Willing 65
Worlds Apart 66
You Made a Choice.. 67
Your Presence.. 68

This collection is dedicated towards all the people who have lost a deep love, and who are trying to move on one day at a time.

Actions

No matter if they regret their actions,
It won't change what happened.
It won't change the hurt.

Afraid

Time moves in slow motion,
A reluctant tide,
Pulling me away,
Yet I cling to the shoreline,
Fingers dug into the sand,
Afraid to let go,
Afraid to be adrift

Back Together

Just when I thought I couldn't,
I woke up and felt a little less pain
I sat a little taller,
Walked with more pep,
And smiled a bit wider

Just when I thought I never could,
I started to put myself back together

Beating Heart

You ripped my heart from my chest with a knife,
And yet,
My beating heart still aches for you.

Biggest Burden

The biggest burden I've learned to bear
is sowing back the broken pieces to my heart
and not going back to the one that shattered me

Bloomed Anew

In the quiet spaces of my heart,
Where echoes of hurt once lingered,
I found the strength to stitch
each fragmented piece of me
back together

The scars became stories,
The tears turned into rivers of resilience,
And in the gentle dawn of self-love,
I bloomed anew

Daily Tears

Will there ever be a day when I won't cry an ocean for you?
You haven't even shed one tear for me

Deserving Love

I deserve a love,
Not for the battles I've fought,
Or the scars I wear,
But for the simple breaths I take,
This silent song my heart hums

I know this —
We are all worthy of love
Not as a reward,
But as a right,
As the sky deserves the sun and the stars

Distant Hum

In the quiet corners of my heart,
A hollow echoes,
A whisper of your name,
The weight of absence,
A heavy cloak,
Draped over my days

I wander through memories,
Like a ghost in a house once warm,
Now cold,
Each room a museum of us
The laughter that lived here,
Now a distant hum,
Fading into silence

Farewell

To the person who let our love die:
Farewell
I wish you the best

Favorite Regret

The life I thought we had is now a thing of the past,
But I can still taste the moments we shared
Those moments may have turned to ashes,
But you are my favorite regret

Field of Thorns

I thought we were a bed of roses,
But, combined,
We are a field of thorns

Fight

All I wanted was you to fight for me
The way I was willing to fight for you

Finding Myself

While the world still dreams,
I wander through the fog,
Seeking fragments of my soul,
Scattered like stars in the night

I find myself in the rustle of leaves,
In the rhythm of rain,
In the silent spaces between breaths,
Where my essence blooms

Foolish Love

I would have let you shatter my heart one last time
if that meant you would have loved me a little longer
I would have sacrificed my mental health
just to have one extra day spent in your presence
And I do not know if that is love
or pure foolishness

Fragments of Light

In the echoes of of laughter,
Fading but never gone,
In the warmth of a memory,
Tender and unspoken,
I discover fragments of light,
Glimmers of grace
That refuse to be extinguished

So, I gather these moments,
And hold them close,
A reminder that comfort does exist,
Even in the darkest times,
Dawn will always follow the night

Garden of my Heart

In the garden of my heart, your absence blooms
A silent song of longing beneath the moon's soft glow
I water dreams with tears, but love remains a whisper
Unheard by the one whose light I seek to know

Hardest Lesson

One of the hardest lessons in life is learning how to be alone
after comfortably living with someone you thought was your soulmate

Hating Myself

I want to hate you for giving up on us,
But I can't
I can only hate myself for not being the person you needed me to be

Heartbroken

I am heartbroken over a love that didn't exist

Home of Silence

In the stillness of our home,
The echoes of laughter hang
Like forgotten photographs,
Their edges curling with time

We move through rooms
Heavy with the weight of silence,
Each step a reminder
of words left unspoken

Hope

I don't know what tomorrow will bring
I can only hope it will be better than today

Hopeful Pain

I asked myself where the pain hurt most
My heart answered by telling me it was in
the place where I had hope things
would be different

I Rise

From the ashes of yesteryear,
I rise with the dawn,
Unshackling the weight of yesterday's murk
In the cool morning breeze,
I find my durability,
Pushing the horizon further,
With each step,
I carve my path anew,
Embracing the unknown,
Guiding my ruptured heart forward

I Will Miss You

In my silence,
I will miss you
I will always love you,
Even if you don't love me

I'm Healing

I'm healing
I'm forgetting
I'm moving on

But you'll always be someone
who shapes my heart

Intense Pain

Someone once asked me what was the most pain I've ever felt
I replied by saying,
"Healing from somebody who I once thought would heal me."

Lessons

There are time in life when we get what we want
Other times, we get lessons:
Patience, empathy, humility, trust, meaning,
awareness, purpose, clarity, grief, and beauty.
Either way, we win.

Letting Go

In the end,
I had to let you go.
I cannot have faith in a man
who is unsure about me.

Life

The most challenging thing in life is meeting
someone you can't live without,
and then living without them.

Loneliness

My heart aches and bleeds
Some wounds never fully heal
You just learn how to patch up the hole inside your chest
I am lonely without you,
but I was lonely with you too
In the end,
I had to choose which type of loneliness I was willing to live with

Lost Relationship

If someone asks me if I know you,
I'll respond by saying we knew each other once,
but not anymore.

Lost Star

Your love, a ghost of the past,
Lingers in the spaces between dreams,
A lost star in the vast expanse,
Still shines in the dark

Love

If you're waiting for someone to love you,
You're probably waiting for something that isn't love
I tell myself this everyday while yearning for you to love me back

Love Lesson

Sometimes,
Love turns out to be nothing more than a lesson

Loving You

I suppose I'll have to keep on loving you
until someone gives my soul what you could not

Memory

One day,
Your sadness will be but a memory

Mosaic of Strength

In the quiet moments of dawn,
Where yesterday's shadows dissolve,
I find the fragments of my heart,
Once shattered, now a mosaic of strength

The wounds, once raw, now fade
Each scar is a story and a lesson

I walk forward, not to forget,
But to remember with grace,
To embrace the sunlight of now,
And the promise of tomorrow

Navigating Sorrow

The world moves on,
Oblivious to my grief,
And I am left to navigate this sorrow alone,
Wading through the wreckage,
Piecing together fragments of a heart once whole

In this desolate landscape,
I find strange solace,
A comfort in the depth of my pain,
For it is all that remains of you,
A testament to a love that burned bright,
And left me in cinders

New Beginnings

In the quiet,
I find the strength to let go,
To release you into the unknown

We part ways,
Carrying the fragments
of a life once intertwined,
Now unraveling into the threads
of two new beginnings

Nightmare of Reality

Did you ever truly love me?
I soak my pillows wet at night thinking about the life we could have had
My dreams are a beautiful world where we are happy,
And then I wake to my nightmare of reality

Not at Fault

I see the pieces, scattered,
Like fallen leaves,
Whispering truths
I dared not hear

The mirror tells stories,
Not of blame, but of freedom,
The weight lifting,
Like mist in the morning light

I am the storm's eye,
Calm, unbroken,
The echoes of fault fading,
Into the vast expanse of sky

Here, in the stillness,
I understand:
I am whole, despite the fracturing,
Not at fault,
And I deserve a love that's real

Old Love Letter

It is a sad thought to think
I will be nothing more than an old love letter
stashed away in a box of your past

Plastered Smile

I see you hanging out with friends
Laughing like you don't have a care in the world
So, I plaster on a smile and swallow my salty tears

Reliving Pain

In the act of moving on,
You relive pain each day
until there is nothing left to feel

Resilience

One thing I've always admired about you is your strength and resilience
But, I feel like I wasn't enough of a reason for you to keep that resilience
Your strength was weakened when you gave up on us

Rough Waters

I had dived into our love headfirst without testing the waters
Turns out, I never learned how to swim,
And I was treading in rough waters until I ran out of breath

Saying Goodbye

The hardest time in your life will be when you have to say goodbye
when
you don't have the strength to let go

Shattered Love

Our love, a fragile thing,
Shattered on the rocks of reality,
It's pieces scattered,
And impossible to gather

We gaze into the abyss
at our separate futures,
Knowing our time together has come to an end

Nothing can restore broken glass

Shipwreck

I am a shipwreck,
Splintered and broken,
Adrift on an ocean of loss,
Searching for a shore
that does not exist
Your love was my anchor,
And now,
I am drifting

Slipping Away

I reach out,
Fingers trembling,
To touch the hand I once held
so tightly, so surely

But your fingers slip away,
Like sand through an hourglass,
Each grain a moment
we can never reclaim

Stark Reality

Nights stretch endlessly,
The moon a witness to my sorrow,
It's light a cruel reminder
of what was,
And what will never be again
Sleep eludes me,
Dreams dissolve into shadows,
And I wake to the stark reality
that you are gone

Storm of Chaos

We thought we would sail off into the sea with a love as strong as the ocean
Little did we know our boat floated into a storm of chaos,
Nearly drowning in the ferocious waves while dodging lightning

Strangers

I do not wish that we never met,
but, in order to heal,
we must become strangers again

Struggling

I know there is no going back,
but my legs are struggling to move forward

Struggling Heart

My heart struggles with loving you, hating you, and letting you go all at
the
same time.

Stuck

All too soon,
I was stuck between wanting to wait for you
and needing to forget you

I couldn't figure out which one was better
And, somehow,
I was doing both at the same time

Tempest of Tears

In the daylight,
I wear a mask of composure,
a facade of normalcy,
but beneath,
a storm rages,
a tempest of tears,
waiting to spill, waiting to flood.

Thank You

To the one who broke my heart:
Thank you for letting me go
Because I would have never walked away

The Wrong Person

You, a shadow in the morning light,
A whisper of a storm,
Your touch, a winter's breath
on the edge of summer.
I loved you, knowing the ache
of petals falling.
Of waves crashing on silent shores,
Of the moon sighing alone in a starless night
Your name, a wound that never heals,
A song that haunts the quiet,
A dream that fades with the dawn.
In the garden of my heart,
You were the thorn among roses,
The tempest in a sea of calm,
And still, I held on,
Loving the wrong person
Like a moth to the flame,
Burning, but never letting go.

There for You

No matter how I feel,
I will always be good to you.
No matter how hard I cry,
I will always mask my pain.
I will be there for you when nobody
is by your side.
I hope this makes you understand
how much I love you.

Tragedy

I loved you more than I ever loved myself,
What a tragedy that turned out to be.

Two Souls

I wanted so badly to fix us,
but we were two souls meant to collide.
For a brief moment,
you made me feel something beautiful.

Unwavering Beauty

The moon, pale and steadfast,
casts its gentle glow
upon the broken edges of hope,
a reminder that even in darkness,
there is a quiet, unwavering beauty.

Willing

I hurt,
I cried,
And we argued.

Yet I was still willing to be yours forever.

Worlds Apart

Your eyes, once bright,
now reflect a distant shore,
a place where love's warmth
has ebbed with the tide.

I trace the line of your face
in the dim light,
mapping the geography of a heart
that no longer beats with mine.

We sit together,
yet worlds apart,
the space between us
a chasm filled with what-ifs and maybes.

You Made a Choice

I don't want to dwell on the past—
but I do.
I don't want to care—
yet, my heart does.
You made a choice.
It wasn't me.
Why was I not enough?

Your Presence

Your presence is everywhere:
In our children,
The book you gave me that is our favorite story,
The video games you taught me to love,
A homemade recipe we loved to share,
A blanket you bought me for our anniversary,
Or a scented candle that smells of the forest.
But, most of all, your presence is trapped in my memories.
Making me miss you more by each passing day.

Don't miss out!

Visit the website below and you can sign up to receive emails whenever Brittany Benko publishes a new book. There's no charge and no obligation.

https://books2read.com/r/B-A-MBYL-PAEBF

BOOKS 2 READ

Connecting independent readers to independent writers.

Also by Brittany Benko

Poetic Poetry: A Short Collection of Poems
Poetic Poems and Prose
The Guiding Pen
Fragments of Us

Watch for more at https://brittanybenko.wixsite.com/booksbybrittany.

About the Author

Brittany is a self-published poet, Hubpages writer, Medium blogger,, LitPick book reviewer, and special needs mother who lives in the Lowcountry of South Carolina. She has been featured in a few anthologies and has been featured as a poet through Spillwords, The Writers Club, The Open-Door Poetry Magazine, the Autism Parenting Magazine, and Poetic Reveries.

Be sure to leave Brittany a review on Goodreads or Bookbub if you enjoyed her book!

Read more at https://brittanybenko.wixsite.com/booksbybrittany.